96 Bars of
Success

Brief History of Music

Dominion Oludayo

PAGE PUBLISHING, INC.
Conneaut Lake, PA

First originally published by Page Publishing 2021

ISBN 978-1-6624-3545-4 (pbk)
ISBN 978-1-6624-3546-1 (digital)

Printed in the United States of America

Glossary

Word	Meaning
(No)	Number
Bar (No)	First line of our line bar
Bar	A structured sentence in a song
Project (No)	The number of the project you are currently working on
Attempt (No)	Amount of times project has been repeated
Freestyle	Written down version of student independent extracurricular work
Title	Name of project

Exercise

BRIEF HISTORY OF MUSIC

Music is found in every known society, past and present, and is considered to be culturally universal.

Since all people of the world, including the most isolated tribal groups, have a form of music, it may be concluded that music is likely to have been present in the ancestral population prior to the dispersal of humans around the world; consequently, the first music may have been invented in Africa, and they involved to become a fundamental constituent of human life, using various materials make various instruments. Culture is music influenced by all other aspect of that culture, including social and economic, originating and experience climate access to technology and what religion is believed.

The emotions and ideas that music expresses, the situations in which music is played and listened to, and attitude toward music players and composers all varies between regions and periods. Music history is the district subfield of musicology and history, which studies music (particularly Western art music) from a chronological perspective.

DATE:	**JOT**	PT:
		TE:
		BT:

	IDEA:
	IDEA:
	IDEA:

Hit That Paper

The "Jot" page is where initial ideas are written down. There are three idea sections for three pages for each project. In the top right corner, write the project details.

	Project No:	
	BAR1:	
	BAR2:	
	BAR3:	
	BAR4:	
	BAR5:	
	BAR6:	
	BAR7:	
	BAR8:	

Bar (No): The first line of a four-line bar. There are eight bar (no) on a page. Meaning, there are thirty-two bars on each page, three pages per project. Therefore, you have ninety-six bars for each project.

Teacher Comment:

Hit That Paper

Freestyle: Express Yourself

In the first section of the blank page, the teacher gives feedback. In the second half, student expresses creativity by writing down their own freestyle.

Glossary of Musical Terms

A

Absolute music: Instrumental music with no intended story (non-programmatic music).

A cappella: Choral music with no instrumental accompaniment.

Accelerando: Gradually speeding up the speed of the rhythmic beat.

Accent: Momentarily emphasizing a note with a dynamic attack.

Adagio: A slow tempo.

Allegro: A fast tempo.

Alto: A low-ranged female voice; the second lowest instrumental range.

Andante: Moderate tempo (a walking speed; "Andare" means to walk).

Aria: A beautiful manner of solo singing, accompanied by orchestra, with a steady metrical beat.

Art music: A general term used to describe the "formal concert music" traditions of the West, as opposed to "popular" and "commercial music" styles.

Art song (genre): A musical setting of artistic poetry for solo voice accompanied by piano (or orchestra).

Atonality: Modern harmony that intentionally avoids a tonal center (has no apparent home key).

Augmentation: Lengthening the rhythmic values of a fugal subject.

Avant-garde ("at the forefront"): A French term that describes highly experimental modern musical styles

B

Ballet (genre): A *programmatic* theatrical work for dancers and orchestra.

Bar: A common term for a musical measure.

Baritone: A moderately low male voice; in range between a tenor and a bass.

Baroque era, c. 1600–1750: A musical period of extremely ornate and elaborate approaches to the arts. This era saw the rise of instrumental music, the invention of the modern violin family, and the creation of the first orchestras (Vivaldi, Handel, JS Bach).

Bass: The lowest male voice; (see double bass).

Bass drum: The lowest-sounding nonpitched percussion instrument.

Basso continuo: The backup ensemble of the Baroque era, usually comprised of a keyboard instrument (harpsichord or organ) and a melodic stringed bass instrument (viola da gamba or cello).

Bassoon: The lowest-sounding regular instrument of the woodwind family (a double-reed instrument).

Beat: A musical pulse.

Bebop: A complex, highly-improvisatory style of jazz promoted by Charlie Parker in the 1940s–'50s.

"Big Band" jazz: See "Swing."

Binary form: A form comprised of two distinctly opposing sections ("A" versus "B").

Bitonality: Modern music sounding in two different keys simultaneously.

Blues: A melancholy style of Afro-American secular music, based on a simple musical/poetic form. "Delta" blues began in the early 1900s; "Classic" blues in the late 1920s; "Rhythm and Blues" in the 1940s.

Brass instrument: A powerful metallic instrument with a mouthpiece and tubing that must be blown into by the player, such as trumpet, trombone, French horn, tuba, baritone, bugel.

DATE:	JOT	Project:
		Title:
		Beat:

IDEA:

_____
_____
_____
_____
_____
_____
_____

IDEA:

_____
_____
_____
_____
_____
_____
_____
_____

IDEA:

_____
_____
_____
_____
_____
_____
_____

Hit This Paper

	Project No:	Title:
		Beat:
		Attempt:
BAR1		
•		
•		
•		
BAR2		
•		
•		
•		
BAR3		
•		
•		
•		
BAR4		
•		
•		
•		
BAR5		
•		
•		
•		
BAR6		
•		
•		
•		
BAR7		
•		
•		
•		
BAR8		
•		
•		
•		

		Title:
	Project No:	Beat:
		Attempt:
BAR1		
•		
•		
•		
BAR2		
•		
•		
•		
BAR3		
•		
•		
•		
BAR4		
•		
•		
•		
BAR5		
•		
•		
•		
BAR6		
•		
•		
•		
BAR7		
•		
•		
•		
BAR8		
•		
•		
•		

	Project No:	Title:
		Beat:
		Attempt:

BAR1	
•	
•	
•	
BAR2	
•	
•	
•	
BAR3	
•	
•	
•	
BAR4	
•	
•	
•	
BAR5	
•	
•	
•	
BAR6	
•	
•	
•	
BAR7	
•	
•	
•	
BAR8	
•	
•	
•	

Teacher Comment:

Hit That Paper

Freestyle: Express Yourself

C

Cadence: A melodic or harmonic punctuation mark at the end of a phrase, major section, or entire work.

Cadenza: An unaccompanied section of virtuosic display played by a soloist in a concerto.

Call and response: A traditional African process in which a leader's phrase ("call") is repeatedly answered by a chorus. This process became an important aspect of many Afro-American styles.

Canon: A type of strict imitation created by strict echoing between a melodic "leader" and subsequent "follower[s]."

Cantata (genre): A composition in several movements, written for chorus, soloist(s), and orchestra; traditionally, these are religious works.

Cello: The tenor-ranged instrument of the modern string family (an abbreviation for *violoncello*).

Chamber music (genre): Music performed by a small group of players (one player per part).

Chance music (genre): A modern manner of composition in which some or all the work is left to chance.

Chant (genre): A monophonic melody sang in a free rhythm (such as "Gregorian" chant of the Roman Catholic Church).

Character piece (genre): A one-movement *programmatic* work for a solo pianist.

Chimes: A percussion instrument comprised of several tube-shaped bells struck by a leather hammer.

Chorale: (1) A Lutheran liturgical melody; (2) a four-part hymn-like chorale harmonization.

Chord: A harmonic combination that has three or more pitches sounding simultaneously.

Chorus: (1) A fairly large choral group; (2) in jazz, a single statement of the main harmonic/melody pattern.

Chromaticism: (1) Harmonic or melodic movement by half-step intervals; (2) harmony that uses pitches beyond the central key of a work.

Clarinet: The tenor-ranged instrument of the woodwind family (a single-reed).

Classical era, c. 1750–1820: A politically turbulent era focused on structural unity, clarity, and balance (Haydn, Mozart, Beethoven).

Coda (means "tail" in Italian): A concluding section appended to the end of a work.

Collegium musicum: A university ensemble dedicated to the performance of early music (pre-1750).

Computer music: Music in which the composition and/or performance is controlled by a computer.

Concert band: A large (nonmarching) ensemble of woodwind, brass, and percussion instruments.

Concerto (genre): The general term for a multimovement work for soloist(s) and orchestra (see "solo concerto" and "concerto grosso").

Concerto grosso (genre): A three-movement work for a small group of soloists and orchestra.

Conductor: The leader of a performing group of musicians.

Consonance: A pleasant-sounding harmony.

Contrabassoon: The lowest-sounding double-reed instrument of the woodwind family.

Cool jazz: A relaxed style of modern jazz, promoted in the 1950s/'60s by Brubeck, etc.

Cornet: A mellow-sounding member of the trumpet family.

Countermelody: A secondary melodic idea that accompanies and opposes a main thematic idea.

Counterpoint: A complex polyphonic texture combining two or more independent melodies.

Crescendo: Gradually getting louder.

Cymbals: Percussion instrument usually consisting of two circular brass plates struck together as a pair.

DATE:	JOT	Project:
		Title:
		Beat:

IDEA:

IDEA:

IDEA:

Hit This Paper

	Project No:	Title:
		Beat:
		Attempt:
BAR1		
•		
•		
•		
BAR2		
•		
•		
•		
BAR3		
•		
•		
•		
BAR4		
•		
•		
•		
BAR5		
•		
•		
•		
BAR6		
•		
•		
•		
BAR7		
•		
•		
•		
BAR8		
•		
•		
•		

	Project No:	Title:
		Beat:
		Attempt:
BAR1		
•		
•		
•		
BAR2		
•		
•		
•		
BAR3		
•		
•		
•		
BAR4		
•		
•		
•		
BAR5		
•		
•		
•		
BAR6		
•		
•		
•		
BAR7		
•		
•		
•		
BAR8		
•		
•		
•		

		Title:
	Project No:	Beat:
		Attempt:
BAR1		
•		
•		
•		
BAR2		
•		
•		
•		
BAR3		
•		
•		
•		
BAR4		
•		
•		
•		
BAR5		
•		
•		
•		
BAR6		
•		
•		
•		
BAR7		
•		
•		
•		
BAR8		
•		
•		
•		

Teacher Comment:

Hit That Paper

Freestyle: Express Yourself

D

Da capo (Italian "to the head"): A written indication telling a performer to go back to the start of a piece.

Decrescendo: Gradually getting quieter (see diminuendo).

Development: (1) The central dramatic section of a sonata form that moves harmonically through many keys; (2) the process of expanding or manipulation a musical idea.

Diatonic: A melody or harmony based on one of the seven-tone major or minor Western scales.

Dies Irae: A chant from the Requiem Mass dealing with God's wrath on the day of judgment.

Diminuendo: Gradually getting quieter (see decrescendo).

Diminution: The shorten the note values of a theme (usually to render it twice as fast).

Decrescendo: Gradually getting quieter (see diminuendo).

Disjunct: A melody that is not smooth in contour (has many leaps).

Doctrine of affections: The Baroque methodology for evoking a specific emotion through music and text.

Dotted note: A written note with a dot to the right of it (the dot adds half the rhythmic duration to the note's original value).

Double bass: The lowest-sounding instrument of the modern string family.

Downbeat: The first beat of a musical measure (usually accented more strongly than other beats).

Duple meter: A basic metrical pattern having two beats per measure.

Dynamics: The musical element of relative musical loudness or quietness

E

Electric instrument: An instrument whose sound is produced or modified by an electromagnetic pickup.

Electronic instrument: An instrument whose sound is produced or modified by electronic means.

English horn: A tenor oboe; a richly nasal-sounding double-reed woodwind instrument.

Ensemble: A group of musical performers.

Episode: An intermediary (contrasting) section of a Baroque fugue or classic rondo form.

Equal temperament: The standard modern tuning system in which the octave is divided into twelve equal "half steps."

Étude (French): A "study" piece, designed to help a performer master a particular technique.

Exposition: (1) The opening section of a fugue; (2) the opening section of a classic sonata form (in which the two opposing key centers are exposed to the listener for the first time).

Expressionism: An ultra-shocking, highly dissonant modern style of music.

F

Falsetto: A vocal technique that allows a male to sing in a much higher, lighter register (by vibrating only half of the vocal cord).

Flat sign (♭): A musical symbol that lowers the pitch one half step.

Flute: A metal tubular instrument that is the soprano instrument of the standard woodwind family.

Form: The elemental category describing the shape/design of a musical work or movement.

Film music (genre): Music that serves either as background or foreground material for a movie.

Forte (f): A loud dynamic marking.

DATE:	**JOT**	Project:
		Title:
		Beat:

IDEA:

IDEA:

IDEA:

Hit This Paper

	Project No:	Title:
		Beat:
		Attempt:
BAR1		
•		
•		
•		
BAR2		
•		
•		
•		
BAR3		
•		
•		
•		
BAR4		
•		
•		
•		
BAR5		
•		
•		
•		
BAR6		
•		
•		
•		
BAR7		
•		
•		
•		
BAR8		
•		
•		
•		

	Project No:	Title:
		Beat:
		Attempt:
BAR1		
•		
•		
•		
BAR2		
•		
•		
•		
BAR3		
•		
•		
•		
BAR4		
•		
•		
•		
BAR5		
•		
•		
•		
BAR6		
•		
•		
•		
BAR7		
•		
•		
•		
BAR8		
•		
•		
•		

		Title:
	Project No:	Beat:
		Attempt:

	BAR1
	•
	•
	•
	BAR2
	•
	•
	•
	BAR3
	•
	•
	•
	BAR4
	•
	•
	•
	BAR5
	•
	•
	•
	BAR6
	•
	•
	•
	BAR7
	•
	•
	•
	BAR8
	•
	•
	•

Teacher Comment:

Hit That Paper

Freestyle: Express Yourself

Fortepiano: An early prototype of the modern piano (designed to play both "loud" and "quiet").

Fortissimo (□): A very loud dynamic marking.

French horn: A valved brass instrument of medium/medium-low range (alto to bass).

Fugue: A complex contrapuntal manipulation of a musical *subject*.

Fusion: A blending of jazz and rock styles.

G

Gamelan: An Indonesian musical ensemble comprised primarily of percussion instruments.

Genre: A category of musical composition (the specific classification of a musical work).

Glissando: A rapid slide between two distant pitches.

Glockenspiel: A pitched-percussion instrument comprised of metal bars in a frame struck by a mallet.

Gong (also called "tam-tam"): A nonpitched percussion instrument made of a large metal plate struck with a mallet

Grave: A slow, solemn tempo.

Gregorian chant (genre): Monophonic, nonmetered melodies set to Latin sacred texts.

Guitar: A six-stringed fretted instrument.

H

Habanera: An exotic Cuban dance in duple meter.

Half step: The smallest interval in the Western system of equal temperament.

Harmony: The elemental category describing vertical combinations of pitches.

Harp: A plucked instrument having strings stretched on a triangular frame.

Harpsichord: An ancient keyboard instrument whose sound is produced by a system of levered picks that pluck its metal strings (common in the Renaissance and Baroque eras).

Home key: *See* tonic key.

Homophonic texture: (1) A main melody supported by chord; (2) a texture in which voices on different pitches sing the same words simultaneously.

Horn: *See* French horn.

Hot jazz: A "Dixieland" style of jazz with a fast tempo promoted by Louis Armstrong.

I

Idée fixe: A transformable melody that recurs in every movement of a multimovement work.

Imitation: A polyphonic texture in which material is presented then echoed from voice to voice.

Impressionism: A modern French musical style based on blurred effects, beautiful tone colors, and fluid rhythms (promoted by Debussy around the turn of the 1900s).

Improvisation: "On-the-spot" creation of music (while it is being performed).

Incidental music (genre): Music performed during a theatrical play.

Instrumentation: the combination of instruments that a composition is written for.

Interval: The measured distance between two musical pitches.

Inversion: A variation technique in which the intervals of a melody are turned upside down.

DATE:	JOT	Project:
		Title:
		Beat:

IDEA:

IDEA:

IDEA:

Hit This Paper

	Project No:	Title:
		Beat:
		Attempt:
BAR1		
•		
•		
•		
BAR2		
•		
•		
•		
BAR3		
•		
•		
•		
BAR4		
•		
•		
•		
BAR5		
•		
•		
•		
BAR6		
•		
•		
•		
BAR7		
•		
•		
•		
BAR8		
•		
•		
•		

	Project No:	Title:
		Beat:
		Attempt:
BAR1		
	•	
	•	
	•	
BAR2		
	•	
	•	
	•	
BAR3		
	•	
	•	
	•	
BAR4		
	•	
	•	
	•	
BAR5		
	•	
	•	
	•	
BAR6		
	•	
	•	
	•	
BAR7		
	•	
	•	
	•	
BAR8		
	•	
	•	
	•	

	Project No:	Title:
		Beat:
		Attempt:
BAR1		
•		
•		
•		
BAR2		
•		
•		
•		
BAR3		
•		
•		
•		
BAR4		
•		
•		
•		
BAR5		
•		
•		
•		
BAR6		
•		
•		
•		
BAR7		
•		
•		
•		
BAR8		
•		
•		
•		

Teacher Comment:

Hit That Paper

Freestyle: Express Yourself

J

Jazz (genre): A style of American modern popular music, combining African and Western musical traits.

Jazz band: An instrumental ensemble comprised of woodwinds (saxophones and clarinets), brasses (trumpets and trombones), and rhythm section (piano/guitar, bass, and drum set).

K

Kettledrums: See timpani.

Key: The central note, chord, or scale of a musical composition or movement.

Key signature: A series of sharps or flats written on a musical staff to indicate the key of a composition.

Keyboard instrument: Any instrument whose sound is initiated by pressing a series of keys with the fingers; piano, harpsichord, organ, synthesizer are the most common types.

Koto: A Japanese plucked instrument with thirteen strings and moveable bridges.

L

Largo: A very slow, broad tempo.

Legato: A smooth, connected manner of performing a melody.

Leitmotif: A short musical "signature tune" associated with a person or concept in a Wagnerian Musikdrama.

Libretto: The sang/spoken text of an opera.

Lied (genre): A German-texted art song (usually for one voice with piano accompaniment); plural = Lieder.

Lute: An ancient pear-shaped plucked instrument widely used in the Renaissance and Baroque eras.

M

Madrigal (genre): A composition on a short secular poem, sang by a small group of unaccompanied singers (one on a part). The madrigal flourished in Italy from 1520 to 1610 and was adopted in England during the Elizabethan age (c. 1600).

Major key: Music based on a major scale (traditionally considered "happy" sounding).

Major scale: A family of seven alphabetically ordered pitches within the distance of an octave, following an intervallic pattern, matching the white keys from "C" to "C" on a piano.

Marching band: A large ensemble of woodwinds, brass, and percussion used for entertainment at sporting events and parades (usually performing marchlike music in a strong duple meter).

Marimba: A pitched percussion instrument comprised of wooden bars struck by mallets.

Mass (genre): In music, a composition based on the five daily prayers of the Roman Catholic Mass ordinary: *kyrie, gloris, credo, Sanctus, Agnus Dei.*

Mass ordinary: The five daily prayers of the Catholic Mass: *kyrie, gloris, credo, Sanctus, Agnus Dei.*

Mass proper: The approximately two dozen prayers of a Mass that change each day to reflect the particular feast day of the liturgical calendar.

Marimba: A pitched percussion instrument comprised of wooden bars struck by mallets; a mellower version of the xylophone.

Mazurka: A type of Polish dance in triple meter, sometimes used by Chopin in his piano works.

DATE:	JOT	Project: Title: Beat:

IDEA:

IDEA:

IDEA:

Hit This Paper

	Project No:	Title:
		Beat:
		Attempt:
BAR1		
•		
•		
•		
BAR2		
•		
•		
•		
BAR3		
•		
•		
•		
BAR4		
•		
•		
•		
BAR5		
•		
•		
•		
BAR6		
•		
•		
•		
BAR7		
•		
•		
•		
BAR8		
•		
•		
•		

		Title:
	Project No:	Beat:
		Attempt:
BAR1		
•		
•		
•		
BAR2		
•		
•		
•		
BAR3		
•		
•		
•		
BAR4		
•		
•		
•		
BAR5		
•		
•		
•		
BAR6		
•		
•		
•		
BAR7		
•		
•		
•		
BAR8		
•		
•		
•		

		Title:
	Project No:	Beat:
		Attempt:
BAR1		
•		
•		
•		
BAR2		
•		
•		
•		
BAR3		
•		
•		
•		
BAR4		
•		
•		
•		
BAR5		
•		
•		
•		
BAR6		
•		
•		
•		
BAR7		
•		
•		
•		
BAR8		
•		
•		
•		

Teacher Comment:

Hit That Paper

Freestyle: Express Yourself

Exercise

Instruction: Fill in the song with a chorus and a bridge to the below lyrics using the four-count signature, given at the exercise instruction, page 4.

Beat tirrte: Trap

Description: The bass drum comes in the first count and south count while the snare comes in the third and seventh count, (see page 4 for example of an eight count)

Champion

Verse 1:

> Am the man of the match
> am the man of the games
> Anywhere I step in, they put up a race
> At the end of the day, I end up been chase
> Looking for space to hang the etranis.

Chorus:

————————————————
———————————————— } 2ce
————————————————

Chorus:

————————————————
———————————————— } Repeatedly
————————————————

Measure: A rhythmic grouping, set off in written music by a vertical bar line.

Medieval: A term used to describe things related to the Middle Ages (c. 450–1450).

Melisma: A succession of many pitches sang while sustaining one syllable of text.

Melody: The musical element that deals with the horizontal presentation of pitch.

Meter: Beats organized into recurring and recognizable accent patterns (2/4, 3/4, 4/4, etc.).

Metronome: A mechanical (or electric) device that precisely measures tempo.

Measure: A rhythmic grouping, set off in written music by a vertical bar line.

Mezzo: An Italian prefix that means "medium."

Mezzo forte *(mf)*: A medium loud dynamic marking.

Mezzo piano (/): A medium quiet dynamic marking.

Mezzo soprano: A dramatic woman's voice that combines the power of an alto with the primary high range of a soprano.

Microtone: A non-Western musical interval that is smaller than a Western half step.

Middle Ages, c. 450–1450: An era dominated by Catholic sacred music, which began as simple *chant* but grew in complexity in the thirteenth to fifteenth centuries by experiments in harmony and rhythm (anonymous monks, PCfotin, Machaut).

MIDI: An acronym for Musical Instrument Digital Interface; a protocol established in the 1970s that allows digital synthesizers to communicate with computers.

Minimalism: A modern compositional approach promoted by Glass, Reich, etc., in which a short melodic/ rhythmic/harmonic idea is repeated and gradually transformed as the basis of an extended work.

Minor key: Music based on a minor scale (traditionally considered "sad" sounding).

Minor scale: A family of seven alphabetically ordered pitches within the distance of an octave, following an intervallic pattern matching the white keys from "A" to "A" on a piano.

Minuet: An aristocratic dance in 3/4 meter.

Minuet and trio form: The traditional third-movement form of the classic four-movement design, based on an aristocratic dance in 3/4 meter.

Mode: A scale or key used in a musical composition (major and minor are modes, as are ancient modal scales found in Western music before c. 1680.

Moderato: A moderate tempo.

Modern Era, c. 1890–present: A musical era impacted by daring experimentation, advances in musical technology, and popular/non-Western influences (Debussy, Schoenberg, Stravinsky, Copland, Cage).

Modulation: The process of changing from one musical key to another.

Monophonic texture: A single-line texture with no harmony.

Motet: A polyphonic vocal piece set to a sacred Latin text that is *not* from the Roman Catholic Mass.

Motive: A small musical fragment ("Lego" block) used to build a larger musical idea; can be reworked in the course of a composition (as in the four-note motive in Beethoven's *Symphony No. 5 in C minor*).

Movement: A complete, independent division of a larger work.

Mp3: A modern technology that allows digital CD-quality sound to be compressed into files that are approximately eight times smaller than the original with no loss of quality.

Musikdrama (genre): A type of ultradramatic German operatic theater developed by Richard Wagner in the mid-/late Romantic era

Musique concrete (genre): Music comprised of natural sounds that are recorded and/or manipulated electronically or via magnetic tape; a compositional approach promoted by Varése in the 1950s.

Mute: A device used to muffle the tone and volume of an instrument.

DATE:	JOT	Project:
		Title:
		Beat:

IDEA:
_____
_____
_____
_____
_____
_____
_____

IDEA:
_____
_____
_____
_____
_____
_____
_____

IDEA:
_____
_____
_____
_____
_____
_____
_____

Hit This Paper

	Project No:	Title:
		Beat:
		Attempt:
BAR1		
•		
•		
•		
BAR2		
•		
•		
•		
BAR3		
•		
•		
•		
BAR4		
•		
•		
•		
BAR5		
•		
•		
•		
BAR6		
•		
•		
•		
BAR7		
•		
•		
•		
BAR8		
•		
•		
•		

	Project No:	Title:
		Beat:
		Attempt:
BAR1		
•		
•		
•		
BAR2		
•		
•		
•		
BAR3		
•		
•		
•		
BAR4		
•		
•		
•		
BAR5		
•		
•		
•		
BAR6		
•		
•		
•		
BAR7		
•		
•		
•		
BAR8		
•		
•		
•		

		Title:
	Project No:	Beat:
		Attempt:
BAR1		
•		
•		
•		
BAR2		
•		
•		
•		
BAR3		
•		
•		
•		
BAR4		
•		
•		
•		
BAR5		
•		
•		
•		
BAR6		
•		
•		
•		
BAR7		
•		
•		
•		
BAR8		
•		
•		
•		

Teacher Comment:

Hit That Paper

Freestyle: Express Yourself

N

Nationalism: Musical styles that include folk songs, dances, legends, language, or other national imagery relating to a composer's native country

Natural sign: A musical symbol that raises the pitch one half step.

Neoclassicism: An early twentieth-century compositional style in which classic forms and the aesthetics of balance, clarity, and structural unity are combined with modern approaches to harmony, rhythm, and tone color.

New age: A style of popular music in the 1980s/'90s that rejected the hard-edged beat of rock music by focusing on nature sounds, sweet synthesized tone colors, acoustic instruments, and short hypnotically repetitive ideas.

Nocturne (French for "night piece"): A type of character piece for solo piano that evokes the moods and images of nighttime.

Nonmetrical: Music without a regular beat or steady meter (you cannot tap your foot to the beat).

Non-Western music: Music from countries other than Europe and the Americas.

Notation: A system for writing music down so that critical aspects of its performance can be recreated accurately.

Note: In music notation, a black or white oval-shaped symbol (with or without a stem/flag) that represents a specific rhythmic duration and/or pitch.

O

Oboe: A nasal-sounding double-reed instrument that is the alto of the standard woodwind family.

Octave: A musical interval between two pitches in which the upper pitch vibrates twice as fast as the lower.

Opera (genre): A large-scale, fully-staged dramatic theatrical work involving solo singers, chorus, and orchestra.

Opera buffa (genre): Comic Italian opera (usually in two acts).

Opera seria (genre): Serious Italian opera (usually in three acts).

Oratorio (genre): A large-scale sacred work for solo singers, chorus, and orchestra that is *not* staged.

Orchestra: A large instrumental ensemble comprised of strings, woodwinds, brasses, and percussion.

Orchestration: The technique of conceiving or arranging a composition for orchestra.

Ordinary: See "Mass Ordinary."

Organ: A wind/keyboard instrument, usually with many sets of pipes controlled from two or more manuals (keyboards), including a set of pedals played by the organist's feet (a set of mechanical or electrical "stops" allow the player to open or close the flow of air to selected groups of pipes).

Organum (genre): A type of early French Medieval polyphony dating from c. 1000–1200, featuring a slow nonmetered chant in the lowest voice with one or more faster metrical voices sang above (in melismatic style many notes sang on each syllable of text).

Ostinato: A short rhythmic/melodic idea that is repeated exactly over and over throughout a musical section or work.

Overture (genre): A one-movement orchestral introduction to an opera (Wagner, Bizet, and other composers after 1850 use the term prelude instead to show dramatic unity between the overture and the theatrical drama that follows it).

DATE:		JOT	Project:
			Title:
			Beat:

IDEA:

IDEA:

IDEA:

Hit This Paper

		Title:
	Project No:	Beat:
		Attempt:
BAR1		
	•	
	•	
	•	
BAR2		
	•	
	•	
	•	
BAR3		
	•	
	•	
	•	
BAR4		
	•	
	•	
	•	
BAR5		
	•	
	•	
	•	
BAR6		
	•	
	•	
	•	
BAR7		
	•	
	•	
	•	
BAR8		
	•	
	•	
	•	

	Project No:	Title:
		Beat:
		Attempt:

	BAR1
	•
	•
	•
	BAR2
	•
	•
	•
	BAR3
	•
	•
	•
	BAR4
	•
	•
	•
	BAR5
	•
	•
	•
	BAR6
	•
	•
	•
	BAR7
	•
	•
	•
	BAR8
	•
	•
	•

DOMINION OLUDAYO

	Project No:	Title:
		Beat:
		Attempt:
BAR1		
•		
•		
•		
BAR2		
•		
•		
•		
BAR3		
•		
•		
•		
BAR4		
•		
•		
•		
BAR5		
•		
•		
•		
BAR6		
•		
•		
•		
BAR7		
•		
•		
•		
BAR8		
•		
•		
•		

Teacher Comment:

Hit That Paper

Freestyle: Express Yourself

P

Pentatonic scale: A folk or non-Western scale having five different notes within the space of an octave.

Percussion instrument: An instrument on which sound is generated by striking its surface with an object.

Phrase: A small musical unit (subsection of a melody) equivalent to a grammatical phrase in a sentence.

Pianissimo (*pp*): A very quiet dynamic markings.

Piano (dynamic; *p*): A quiet dynamic marking.

Piano (instrument): A versatile modern keyboard instrument that makes sound via fingered keys that engage felt-tipped hammers that strike the strings.

Pianoforte: The original instrumental prototype of the piano (late Baroque / early classic eras).

Pitch: The relative highness or lowness of a musical sound (based on frequency of vibration).

Pizzicato: Usually refers to a type of violin playing in which a string is plucked by the fingers.

Phrase: A small musical unit (subsection of a melody) equivalent to a grammatical phrase in a sentence.

Polka: A lively Bohemian (Czech) dance (traditionally for the common classes).

Polonaise: A Polish nationalistic military dance used in some of Chopin's piano character pieces.

Polyphony: Music with two or more sounds happening simultaneously.

Polyphonic texture: When two or more independent melodic lines are sounding at the same time.

Polyrhythm: When several independent rhythmic lines are sounding at the same time.

Polytonality: When music is played in two or more contrasting keys at the same time.

Postlude: A concluding section (usually at the end of a keyboard movement).

Prelude (genre): (1) A free-form introductory movement to a fugue or other more complex composition; (2) a term used instead of overture (by Wagner, Bizet, and other later Romantic composers) to show dramatic unity between the introductory orchestral music and the theatrical drama that follows it.

Prepared piano: A modern technique invented by John Cage in which various natural objects (spoons, erasers, screws, etc.) are strategically inserted between the strings of a piano in order to create unusual sounds.

Presto: A very fast tempo.

Program music (or "programmatic music") (genre): Instrumental music intended to tell a specific story or set a specific mood or extramusical image.

Program symphony (genre): A programmatic multimovement work for orchestra.

Progression: A series of chords that functions similarly to a sentence or phrase in written language.

Proper (Mass): See Mass proper.

Q

Quadruple meter: A basic metrical pattern having four beats per measure.

Quotation music (genre; common since c. 1960): A composition extensively using quotations from earlier works

R

Raga: A melodic pattern used in the music of India.

Ragtime: A style of piano music developed around the turn of the twentieth century with a marchlike tempo, a syncopated right-hand melody, and an "oompah" left-hand accompaniment.

DATE:		**JOT**	Project:
			Title:
			Beat:

IDEA:
_____
_____
_____
_____
_____
_____

IDEA:
_____
_____
_____
_____
_____
_____
_____

IDEA:
_____
_____
_____
_____
_____
_____
_____

Hit This Paper

	Project No:	Title:
		Beat:
		Attempt:
BAR1		
•		
•		
•		
BAR2		
•		
•		
•		
BAR3		
•		
•		
•		
BAR4		
•		
•		
•		
BAR5		
•		
•		
•		
BAR6		
•		
•		
•		
BAR7		
•		
•		
•		
BAR8		
•		
•		
•		

	Project No:	Title:
		Beat:
		Attempt:
BAR1		
•		
•		
•		
BAR2		
•		
•		
•		
BAR3		
•		
•		
•		
BAR4		
•		
•		
•		
BAR5		
•		
•		
•		
BAR6		
•		
•		
•		
BAR7		
•		
•		
•		
BAR8		
•		
•		
•		

		Title:
	Project No:	Beat:
		Attempt:
BAR1		
•		
•		
•		
BAR2		
•		
•		
•		
BAR3		
•		
•		
•		
BAR4		
•		
•		
•		
BAR5		
•		
•		
•		
BAR6		
•		
•		
•		
BAR7		
•		
•		
•		
BAR8		
•		
•		
•		

Teacher Comment:

Hit That Paper

Freestyle: Express Yourself

Range: The distance between the lowest and highest possible notes of an instrument or melody.

Rap (hip-hop): A style of popular music developed by Afro-Americans in the 1970s in which the lyrics are spoken over rhythm tracks.

Recapitulation: The third aspect of classic sonata form; in this section, both themes of the exposition are restated in the home key (the second theme gives up its opposing key center).

Recitative: A speechlike style of singing with a free *rhythm* over a sparse accompaniment.

Recorder: An ancient wooden flute.

Reed: A flexible strip of cane (or metal) that vibrates in the mouthpiece of a wind instrument.

Register: A specific coloristic portion of an instrumental or vocal range.

Renaissance, c. 1450–1600: An era that witnessed the rebirth of learning and exploration. This was reflected musically in a more personal style than seen in the Middle Ages (Josquin des Prez, Palestrina, Weelkes).

Requiem Mass (genre): A Roman Catholic Mass for the dead.

Retrograde: A melody presented in backward motion.

Retrograde inversion: A melody presented backward and intervalically upside down.

Rhythm: The element of music as it unfolds in time.

Rhythm and blues: A style of Afro-American popular music that flourished in the 1940s–'60s; a direct predecessor to rock and roll.

Ritardando: Gradually slowing down the tempo.

Ritornello form: A Baroque design that alternates big versus small effects (tutti versis solo); usually the tutti section is a recurring melodic refrain.

Rock and roll: A style of popular music that emerged in the 1950s out of the combination of Afro-American, country-Western, and pop-music elements.

Romantic Era, c. 1820–1890: An era of flamboyance, nationalism, the rise of "superstar" performers, and concerts aimed at middle-class-"paying" audiences. Orchestral, theatrical, and soloistic music grew to spectacular heights of personal expression (Schubert, Berlioz, Chopin, Wagner, Brahms, Tchaikovsky).

Rondo form: A classic form in which a main melodic idea returns two or three times in alternation with other melodies (ABACA or ABACABA, etc.).

Rubato: A flexible approach to metered rhythm in which the tempo can be momentarily sped up or slowed down at will for greater personal expression.

S

Sackbut: An ancient brass instrument; ancestor to the trombone.

Saxophone: A family of woodwind instruments with a single reed and brass body; commonly used in jazz and marching band/ concert band music.

Scale: An family of pitches arranged in an ascending/descending order.

Scat singing: A style of improvised jazz singing sang on colorful non-sense syllables.

Scherzo: A country dance in triple meter.

Scherzo and trio form: A musical movement based on a country dance in triple meter; replaced the aristocratic minuet in the early 1800s as the usual third movement of the classic four-movement design.

Sequence: The immediate repetition of a melodic passage on a higher or lower pitch level.

Score: Written notation that vertically aligns all instrumental/vocal parts used in a composition.

DATE:	JOT	Project:
		Title:
		Beat:

IDEA:

IDEA:

IDEA:

Hit This Paper

		Title:
	Project No:	Beat:
		Attempt:
BAR1		
•		
•		
•		
BAR2		
•		
•		
•		
BAR3		
•		
•		
•		
BAR4		
•		
•		
•		
BAR5		
•		
•		
•		
BAR6		
•		
•		
•		
BAR7		
•		
•		
•		
BAR8		
•		
•		
•		

		Title:
	Project No:	Beat:
		Attempt:
BAR1		
	•	
	•	
	•	
BAR2		
	•	
	•	
	•	
BAR3		
	•	
	•	
	•	
BAR4		
	•	
	•	
	•	
BAR5		
	•	
	•	
	•	
BAR6		
	•	
	•	
	•	
BAR7		
	•	
	•	
	•	
BAR8		
	•	
	•	
	•	

DOMINION OLUDAYO

	Project No:	Title:
		Beat:
		Attempt:
BAR1		
•		
•		
•		
BAR2		
•		
•		
•		
BAR3		
•		
•		
•		
BAR4		
•		
•		
•		
BAR5		
•		
•		
•		
BAR6		
•		
•		
•		
BAR7		
•		
•		
•		
BAR8		
•		
•		
•		

Teacher Comment:

Hit That Paper

Freestyle: Express Yourself

Serenade (genre): A classic instrumental chamber work similar to a small-scale symphony; usually performed for social entertainment of the upper classes.

Serialism: A method of modern composition in which the twelve chromatic pitches are put into a numerically ordered series used to control various aspects of a work (melody, harmony, tone color, dynamics, instrumentation, etc.).

Shakuhachi: A Japanese flute.

Shamisen: A banjo-like Japanese stringed instrument.

Sharp sign (#): A musical symbol that raises the pitch one half step.

Shawm: An ancient double-reed woodwind instrument.

Sforzando (□): Sudden stress on a note or chord.

Singspiel (genre): A traditionally low-level type of comic light opera, featuring spoken German dialogue interspersed with simple German songs.

Sitar: A long-necked stringed instrument of India.

Snare drum: A nonpitched drum with two heads stretched over a metal shell; the lower head has metal wires strapped across it to produce a rattling sound.

Solo concerto (genre): A three-movement work for a single soloist versus an orchestra.

Sonata (genre): A classic multimovement work for a piano (or for one instrument with piano accompaniment).

Sonata form (also called sonata-allegro form): The common first-movement form of classic multimovement instrumental works; essentially a musical debate between two opposing key centers characterized by three dramatic structural divisions within a single movement: exposition (two opposing keys are presented); development (harmonically restless); recapitulation (all material is presented in the home key).

Sonata-rondo form: A formal design that combines aspects of sonata form and rondo form: (an ABACABA design in which the opening ABA=exposition (two opposing keys presented in "A" versus "BA"); C=development (harmonically restless); the last ABA=recapitulation (all material is presented in the home key).

Song (genre): A small-scale musical work that is sung (a German song is a "Lied"; a French song is a "chanson"; an Italian song is a "canzona").

Song cycle (genre): A set of poetically unified songs (for one singer accompanied by either piano or orchestra).

Soprano: (1) The highest ranged woman's voice or a high prepubescent boy's voice; (2) the highest-sounding instrument of an instrumental family.

Sousaphone: An ultrabass brass instrument designed for use in marching bands.

Sprechstimme: A half-spoken, half-sung style of singing on approximate pitches, developed by Schoenberg in the early 1900s.

Staccato: Short, detached notes.

String instrument: An instrument that is played by placing one's hands directly on the strings, such as violin, viola, cello, double bass, harp, guitar, dulcimer, psaltery, and the ancient viols.

String quartet: (1) A chamber ensemble of two violins, viola, and cello, devised in the early classic era; (2) a multimovement work (genre) for two violins, viola, and cello.

Strophic form: A song form featuring several successive verses of text sung to the same music.

Subject: The main melodic idea of a fugue.

Suite (genre): A collection of dance movements.

Swing: A term to describe "Big Band" jazz music of the 1930s–'50s.

DATE:	JOT	Project:
		Title:
		Beat:

IDEA:

IDEA:

IDEA:

Hit This Paper

		Title:
	Project No:	Beat:
		Attempt:
BAR1		
•		
•		
•		
BAR2		
•		
•		
•		
BAR3		
•		
•		
•		
BAR4		
•		
•		
•		
BAR5		
•		
•		
•		
BAR6		
•		
•		
•		
BAR7		
•		
•		
•		
BAR8		
•		
•		
•		

		Title:
	Project No:	Beat:
		Attempt:
BAR1		
•		
•		
•		
BAR2		
•		
•		
•		
BAR3		
•		
•		
•		
BAR4		
•		
•		
•		
BAR5		
•		
•		
•		
BAR6		
•		
•		
•		
BAR7		
•		
•		
•		
BAR8		
•		
•		
•		

	Project No:	Title:
		Beat:
		Attempt:
BAR1		
•		
•		
•		
BAR2		
•		
•		
•		
BAR3		
•		
•		
•		
BAR4		
•		
•		
•		
BAR5		
•		
•		
•		
BAR6		
•		
•		
•		
BAR7		
•		
•		
•		
BAR8		
•		
•		
•		

Teacher Comment:

Hit That Paper

Freestyle: Express Yourself

Symphonic poem (genre): A single-movement programmatic work for orchestra.

Symphony (genre): A multimovement work for orchestra.

Syncopation: An "off-the-beat" accent.

Synthesizer: A modern electronic keyboard instrument capable of generating a multitude of sounds.

T

Tabla: A pair of drums used to accompany the music of India.

Tala: A rhythmic pattern used in the music of India.

Tempo: The speed of the musical beat.

Tenor: A high-ranged male voice.

Ternary form: ABA design (statement, contrast, restatement).

Texture: The element focusing on the number of simultaneous musical lines being sounded.

Theme: The main self-contained melody of a musical composition.

Theme and variations form: A theme is stated then undergoes a series of sectional alterations.

Through-composed form: A song form with no large-scale musical repetition.

Timbre: Another term for tone color.

Timpani: Various-sized kettle-shaped pitched drums; a tenor instrument of the percussion family.

Tone color: The unique, characteristic sound of a musical instrument or voice.

Tone cluster: A modern technique of extreme harmonic dissonance created by a large block of pitches sounding simultaneously.

Tonality: Music centered around a "home" key (based on a major or minor scale).

Tone row: An ordered series of twelve chromatic pitches used in serialism.

Tonic: The first note of a scale or key.

Tonic key: The "home" key of a tonal composition.

Transition: A bridge section between two musical ideas.

Transposition: Shifting a piece to a different pitch level.

Tremolo: Rapid repetition of a pitch (i.e., bowing a string rapidly while maintaining a constant pitch).

Triad: A three-note chord built on alternating scales steps (1-3-5, etc.).

Trill: Rapid alternation of two close pitches to create a "shaking" ornament on a melodic note.

Trio sonata (genre): A Baroque multimovement chamber work for four performers (two violins and basso continuo).

Triple meter: A common meter with three beats per measure.

Triplet: A rhythmic grouping of three equal-valued notes played in the space of two (indicated in written music by a "3" above the grouping).

Trombone: A family of brass instruments that change pitch via a moveable slide (alto, tenor, and bass versions are common).

Trumpet: A valved instrument that is the soprano of the modern brass family.

Tuba: A large valved brass instrument; the bass of the modern brass family.

Tubular bells: See chimes.

Tutti (Italian for "all" or "everyone"): An indication for all performers to play together.

DATE:	JOT	Project:
		Title:
		Beat:

IDEA:

IDEA:

IDEA:

Hit This Paper

	Project No:	Title:
		Beat:
		Attempt:
BAR1		
•		
•		
•		
BAR2		
•		
•		
•		
BAR3		
•		
•		
•		
BAR4		
•		
•		
•		
BAR5		
•		
•		
•		
BAR6		
•		
•		
•		
BAR7		
•		
•		
•		
BAR8		
•		
•		
•		

	Project No:	Title:
		Beat:
		Attempt:
BAR1		
•		
•		
•		
BAR2		
•		
•		
•		
BAR3		
•		
•		
•		
BAR4		
•		
•		
•		
BAR5		
•		
•		
•		
BAR6		
•		
•		
•		
BAR7		
•		
•		
•		
BAR8		
•		
•		
•		

		Title:
	Project No:	Beat:
		Attempt:
BAR1		
•		
•		
•		
BAR2		
•		
•		
•		
BAR3		
•		
•		
•		
BAR4		
•		
•		
•		
BAR5		
•		
•		
•		
BAR6		
•		
•		
•		
BAR7		
•		
•		
•		
BAR8		
•		
•		
•		

Teacher Comment:

Hit That Paper

Freestyle: Express Yourself

Exercise

Instruction: Fill in the song with a verse 1 and verse 2 to below chorus using the four-count time signature, given at the exercise instruction, page 4.

Beat tittle: Funk

Description: The bass drum comes in on the first count and in between the second and third count while the snare or ctap comes on the second count and fourth count (see page 4 for example of 4 count).

Champion

Verse 1:

_____
_____
_____
_____
_____

Chorus:

> The world is big...
> The world is large...
> for all to share love,
> With one another...

Chorus:

_____
_____
_____
_____
_____

U

'Ūd: A lute-like, pear-shaped, fretless stringed instrument commonly used in music from the Middle East.

Unison: The rendering of a single melodic line by several performers simultaneously.

Upbeat: The weak beat that comes before the strong downbeat of a musical measure.

V

Variation: The compositional process of changing an aspect(s) of a musical work while retaining others.

Verismo: A style of true-to-life Italian opera that flourished at the turn of the twentieth century.

Vibrato: Small fluctuations in pitch used to make a sound more expressive.

Viol: An ancient string instrument (ancestor to the modern violin).

Viola da gamba: A Renaissance bowed string instrument held between the legs like a modern cello.

Viola: The alto instrument of the modern string family.

Violin: The soprano instrument of the modern string family.

Violoncello: The full name of the cello; the tenor instrument of the modern string family.

Virtuoso: A performer of extraordinary ability.

Vivace: A lively tempo.

Volume: The relative quietness or loudness of an electrical impulse (see dynamics).

W

Waltz: An aristocratic ballroom dance in triple meter that flourished in the Romantic period.

Whole step: An interval twice as large as a half step (example: the distance between C and D on a piano).

Whole-tone scale: A scale made of six whole steps that avoids any sense of tonality (example: C D E F# G# A#).

Woodwind instrument: An instrument that produces its sound from a column of air vibrating within a multiholed tube.

Word-painting: In vocal music, musical gestures that reflect the specific meaning of words; a common aspect of the Renaissance madrigal.

World beat: The collective term for today's popular third-world musical styles (also called ethno-pop).

X

Xylophone: A pitched percussion instrument consisting of flat wooden bars on a metal frame that are struck by hard mallets.

DATE:	JOT	Project:
		Title:
		Beat:

IDEA:
_____
_____
_____
_____
_____
_____
_____
_____

IDEA:
_____
_____
_____
_____
_____
_____
_____
_____

IDEA:
_____
_____
_____
_____
_____
_____
_____
_____

Hit This Paper

		Project No:	Title:
			Beat:
			Attempt:
BAR1			
	•		
	•		
	•		
BAR2			
	•		
	•		
	•		
BAR3			
	•		
	•		
	•		
BAR4			
	•		
	•		
	•		
BAR5			
	•		
	•		
	•		
BAR6			
	•		
	•		
	•		
BAR7			
	•		
	•		
	•		
BAR8			
	•		
	•		
	•		

	Project No:	Title:
		Beat:
		Attempt:
BAR1		
•		
•		
•		
BAR2		
•		
•		
•		
BAR3		
•		
•		
•		
BAR4		
•		
•		
•		
BAR5		
•		
•		
•		
BAR6		
•		
•		
•		
BAR7		
•		
•		
•		
BAR8		
•		
•		
•		

	Project No:	Title:
		Beat:
		Attempt:
BAR1		
•		
•		
•		
BAR2		
•		
•		
•		
BAR3		
•		
•		
•		
BAR4		
•		
•		
•		
BAR5		
•		
•		
•		
BAR6		
•		
•		
•		
BAR7		
•		
•		
•		
BAR8		
•		
•		
•		

Teacher Comment:

Hit That Paper

Freestyle: Express Yourself

Exercise

Chorus:

> Who else can flex in a race
> Hit the rate with the baby face
> Baby stepped in the place
> With some flex in a case
>
> Well let's get to the chase
> Do your dance go low to your lace
> Put some check on the waist
> Lost with the hip it's a maze

Verse 1:

Verse 2:

About the Author

D Oludayo and his associates—from paper productions powered by Don money trees—have been able to come up with a book that could potentially influence the educational music system on a very large scale.

They are all in college, and from as long as he can remember, like most kids of their generation, they have all collectively been into music and poetry. It's been one of the tools that has gotten them through their individual challenges in life. It helps as a distraction from reality and to focus the mind at the same time. Some of the questions that led to the foundation idea of the project were, What kid doesn't like music? What child does not listen to music and try to absorb it into their own lifestyle? So since music has become such a major influential factor in the lifestyle of most of this current generation, then why not implement teaching kids how to write it in schools?

CPSIA information can be obtained
at www.ICGtesting.com
Printed in the USA
LVHW092104100721
692238LV00003B/32

9 781662 435454